101 FACTS YOU CAN'T PROVE AREN'T NOT TRUE

Hemmerle | Waldman

D0863548

Hoehn Zone Publications

101 Facts

You Can't Prove
Aren't Not True

101 Facts You Can't Prove Aren't Not True

Illustrations by Alexander Pawlicki

Printed in the United States of America

10 9 8 7 6 5 4 3 2 1

First Printing, 2016

Library of Congress Cataloging-in-Publication Data is available.

ISBN: 978-0-9903548-3-3

Hoehn Zone Publications
Austin, Texas

101 Facts You Can't Prove Aren't Not True

Bed Bath & Beyond is named
for its two founders.

If asked, a cop legally has to tell you what he's having for lunch.

Windmills are entirely
for decoration.

Horses can only do math in base 13.

The great pyramids are the tops of much larger pyramids. Ten new feet of pyramid is excavated annually.

Milli and Vanilli traded names in the middle of recording their third album.

Sheep flock exclusively in prime numbered groups.

The safest place to be in an avalanche is on its left.

In Greek, the letter "J" is jsilent.

The hula-hoop was originally intended for use by two people.

Cows always face east when grazing.

The light bulb predates the discovery of electricity and began life as the "filament isolation bulb."

The surrender of Athens was meant to be sarcastic.

The word "cold sore" means *terrible lizard* in Latin.

NBA players are legally barred from playing carnival games of chance.

If electric eels were capable of surviving in oil, two eels could power an average American home for a year.

Windsocks should be changed daily.

Gift horses will instinctively attack when looked in the mouth.

After the Ford Model T, the second product to be manufactured on an assembly line was the Lazy Susan.

Koalas are highly susceptible to Seasonal Affective Disorder.

Soup spoon volume was
standardized in late 1970's.

The board game Clue is based on actual events.

Cologne was discovered after a Parisian gardener's popularity with women was attributed to a particularly aromatic pesticide.

It's pronounced "vase."

The actor who played Paul on
The Wonder Years went on
to serve two terms as
the UN Secretary-General.

Turkey is cheaper than chicken because chickens are union.

LOCAL HENS UNION
CHAPTER 302

DAYS WITHOUT
ACCIDENT
9

Most people have a mild allergy to salt water.

The closest relative to birds, genetically speaking, is the mild-mannered sea cucumber.

In the original ending of *Old Yeller*, the dog survives, but test audiences found it unbelievable and desired an ending with more pathos.

If shampoo and conditioner are stored together in a sealed container, they explode at room temperature.

If you roll three dice simultaneously, their sum will always equal 13.

(Probably)

Jennifer Love Hewitt took her stage name from a 4th grade valentine mistakenly delivered to her desk.

The "chicken or the egg" debate was laid to rest in 1968.

Water-based paints can be used for nourishment in a survival situation.

You can fit the Great Wall of China in the Hoover Dam.

Reykjavik is named
for its Spanish settler.

The phrase "Tall, dark, and handsome" originated as a selling point in 18th century horse trade.

A word spelled the same backward, forward, and upside down is called a parallellodrome.

Raccoons lack ambition.

The hash marks on your car's gas gauge are arbitrary.

There are more mice in the world than limestone.

A majority of cave paintings
are self-portraits.

Lefties are more sexually active, while righties are more prone to gallstones.

Chartreuse is the only color
that is also a flavor.

Fabric getting darker when wet
is just a coincidence.

For superstitious reasons,
the floors in Las Vegas hotels are
all numbered seven.

Humpback whale promiscuity directly correlates to blowhole diameter.

Charlie Chaplain's signature mustache covered a scar, which agents said would prevent him from "being in the pictures."

10% of parking fees go
to The Red Cross.

Each year, Canada adds a new word to their national anthem.

A few drops of blood can be used to temporarily plug a punctured tire.

Penguins can fly,
but due to weather conditions just
don't see the appeal.

The 911 emergency number was chosen because it's the easiest number to remember.

Salamanders are developmentally disabled lizards.

Shoes strung over power lines kill six Americans annually.

The Eisenhower Interstate System was modeled after the avian circulatory system.

The middle lane of the Autobahn is referred to as "Penny Lane."

The most common dream for dogs
is flying.

A single giant redwood could feed a
family of four for a year.

The phrase "Once you go black…"
is only 60% accurate.

Cattle sleep in shifts.

Veterinarians created "dog years" to comfort despondent canines in existential crises.

The Super Mario Brothers are actually second cousins.

Anti-social salmon
swim downstream.

Both amphibians and reptiles
used to begin with the letter "a,"
however reptiles lost the vowel after
300 million years of evolution.

Subway cannot safely build a sandwich longer than six feet due to salami's critical mass.

A shark's dorsal fin never stops growing, and is constantly being worn down by surface debris.

Roombas have a hidden setting
which, when enabled,
allows them to sense fear.

Crust was added to bread in the 1940's for mothers to use as bargaining chips with obstinate children and finicky eaters.

You can hold your breath for twice as long if you focus your thoughts on clouds, balloons, and other air-related items.

Dreadlocks are worn in tribute to the wooly mammoths that roamed the islands during the Ice Age.

The first person to cross the Pacific Ocean in a barrel almost gave up with less than a mile to go.

Nyquil used to contain Absinthe, before it was removed for contributing to poor neck control and bouts of sleep-karate.

It is impossible to drink from a straw while simultaneously thinking about eating cotton.

Gutenberg created the printing press to meet pre-order demand for the Bible.

Ambulance sirens play
"Shave and a Haircut"
at quarter speed.

The eight reindeer that pull Santa's sleigh are named after German breakfast sandwiches.

The official number for
"Too many cooks in a kitchen"
is nine.

Broken Windows Theory is only metaphorical and does not apply to window vandalism.

Barracuda can only see in the color chrome.

The Mona Lisa was painted as a gift after one of Da Vinci's friends helped him move.

The Zodiac Killer was a Gemini.

Taco Tuesday is
the longest running promotion
in the United States.

Indians were named for the East India Company as part of a corporate branding agreement signed by Christopher Columbus.

It's been renewed every year.

Made in the USA
San Bernardino, CA
18 October 2016